TALKING ABOUT

Death &
Dying

Bruce Sanders

Franklin Watts
London • Sydney

© Aladdin Books Ltd 2003

Designed and produced by
Aladdin Books Ltd
28 Percy Street
London W1T 2BZ

First published in Great Britain
in 2003 by
Franklin Watts
96 Leonard Street
London EC2A 4XD

ISBN: 0 7496 5394 9

Design:
Flick, Book Design and Graphics

Picture research:
Brian Hunter Smart

Consultant:
The consultant, Dr. Heather
Tolliday, is a psychotherapist
who works with children in a
private practice.

The publishers would like to
acknowledge that the
photographs reproduced in this
book have been posed by
models or have been obtained
from photographic agencies.

A CIP record for this book
is available from the
British Library.

Printed in UAE

Contents

"What does death have to do with me?"

You may be like most people and think that death is something which you will not have to face for a long time.

However, it is important to realise that all living things die, and that we all have to deal with death in our lives.

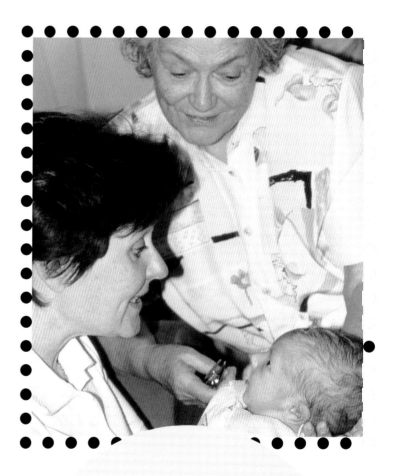

Death is a part of life, just like being born, growing up and growing old.

Most people die when they get old and their body stops working. Death is also caused by a very bad illness or accident. These can happen at any age.

This book talks about death and explains what happens when people die. It also looks at the feelings that you and others may have about death and dying.

"What is death?"

To understand what death is, you first have to know what makes people alive.

When you are alive, you breathe and your heart pumps blood around your body. You can move and your brain senses things going on around you.

Death is the end of life. When someone dies, their heart stops beating, they stop breathing and their brain no longer senses anything.

For most people, death happens peacefully. They die because their bodies are too old to keep on working.

When people get very sick, they also die because their body stops working. When people die in an accident, their body is so badly injured that a doctor can't make it work again.

However, people don't usually die after an accident, getting sick or going to the hospital.

Did you know...

People around the world have many different ideas about what happens when we die. Many people believe that part of us, called our "spirit" or our "soul", carries on living after our body has stopped working. People also go on living in our memories.

"What is dying?"

A dying person is someone who is going to die soon. Most people expect to die when they get old, but some people die earlier because of a bad illness or disease.

However, it can take months or years to die from an illness. Doctors know that the person is dying, but they can't tell how long it will take.

When people have had a happy life, they may not feel sad or upset about dying.

A dying person needs a lot of care and support from those around them. They may feel afraid about dying, or sad about people they are leaving behind. That's why visits from friends and relatives are important to them.

Perhaps you know someone who is dying but you don't want to visit them. That's okay. A phone call can cheer them up, too.

Think about it

It is hard to understand death, even for adults. No one really knows what it is like. But you should know that:

• People do not die because they have been bad.

• Once someone is dead, you cannot bring them back to life, however much you may want to.

• You cannot kill someone by thinking bad things about them.

• Death is not a monster that takes people away. People die because their bodies stop working.

• Death is not like a disease. You cannot catch it from someone else.

"Why are people afraid of death?"

Have you ever had a great holiday and you didn't want it to end? Most people feel like that about living. They want their own lives and those of the people they love to go on and on. The idea of dying can also seem scary. People know that everyone dies one day. They may think, "When will I die?". or "What will it feel like?".

Some people try not to think about death at all. But death is part of everyone's life.

Talking about death can help you to understand it. If you are worried, or have any questions, talk to your Mum or Dad, or another adult that you trust.

Everyone thinks about what will happen when they die.

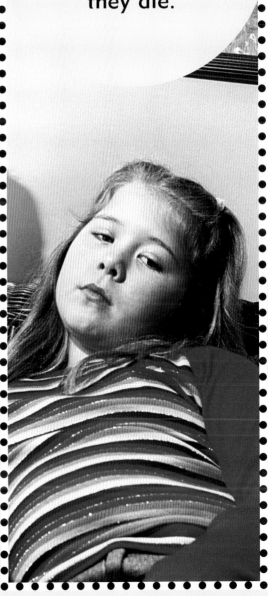

My Story

"I used to worry a lot about what would happen if Mum suddenly died. One day I told Mum what I was thinking. We had a long chat about it. It made me realise that everyone worries about things that probably won't happen for a long time."
Tanya

"What happens to you after you die?"

You will have heard many stories about what happens to you after you die. Many people have strong beliefs about this. Some think it is the end of one life and the start of another. They believe your soul lives on. Some believe your soul goes to heaven. But others believe that when the body dies nothing else happens.

Photos help many people to remember loved ones who have died.

Most people agree that when someone dies, they live on in the memories of the people who loved them.

People remember someone by doing things such as looking at a photo or visiting a place the person loved. Or they keep something special that belonged to the person.

My Story

"When my dog died, I thought, 'It's my fault – he died because I didn't look after him.' Then Mum explained that he just got very ill and his body stopped working. I still miss him lots, but I realise it wasn't my fault that he died."
Andy

"How do people feel when somebody dies?"

When someone dies, their family, friends and other people around them experience grief. This is usually a mix of lots of different feelings. People also grieve in different ways.

If you have lost someone close to you, you may feel sad, angry or shocked, or nothing at all. Your body may hurt or perhaps you feel tired. You may worry about what will happen next.

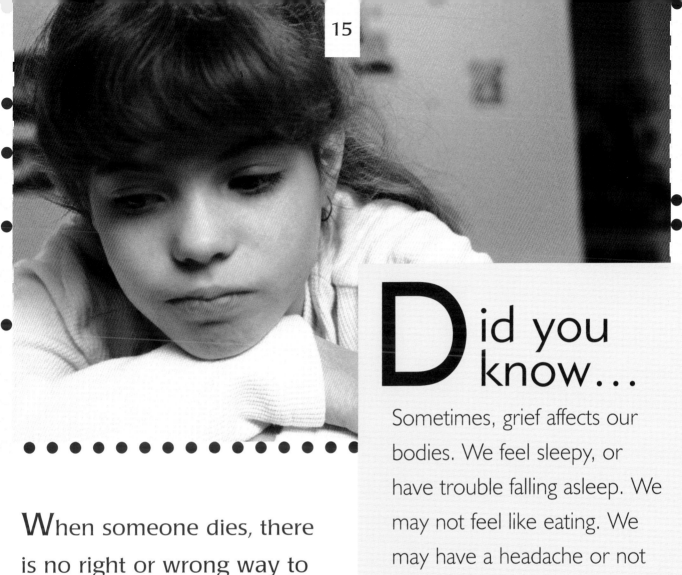

When someone dies, there is no right or wrong way to feel. It's okay if you cry and it's okay if you don't cry.

Different feelings are normal, so don't be afraid to show your feelings to other people.

Did you know...

Sometimes, grief affects our bodies. We feel sleepy, or have trouble falling asleep. We may not feel like eating. We may have a headache or not feel like doing things we usually like to do, such as playing with friends or going to school.

All of these experiences are normal if you have lost someone you cared about.

"What is a funeral?"

A funeral gives people a chance to say good-bye to the person who has died.

In most countries, people are taken to a special place when they die. Their bodies are usually buried in a coffin or cremated (see opposite page).

Often people hold a ceremony, called a funeral. It is a way of saying good-bye to the person who has died. What happens at the funeral depends on people's beliefs.

At a funeral, people come together to remember the dead person and express their grief. A funeral helps them support each other and face up to life.

If someone close to you has died, you may want to take part in the funeral. Ask an adult how you can help.

If you do not want to go to the funeral, that's okay. There are many other ways to remember someone. You could light a candle or say a prayer.

Did you know…

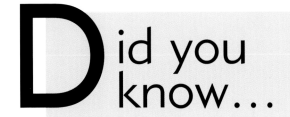

A cremation is when a dead person's body is put in a room that is very hot, until their body turns to soft, powdery ash. Because the person is dead, they cannot feel anything. The ashes are put into jars called urns. Relatives often keep these in a special place to remind them of their loved one.

"How do people deal with grief?"

Once a funeral is over, you may think that life has to get back to normal. But it is not that simple for people who are grieving. Grief can go on for a very long time.

Everyone grieves in their own way. Some people show their feelings right from the start. Other people may not show their feelings for a long time.

Some adults find it hard to show their real feelings. They may only want to cry on their own.

When people are grieving, they may do lots of different things to help them.

Often they will spend hours talking about the person who has died. They may like to remember the good times they had with that person. Or they may read letters that the person wrote to them.

My Story

"After my sister Rosie died, I had lots of feelings all mixed up inside. Some days, I felt angry and wanted to smash my toys. Other times, I felt lonely or guilty. But however I was feeling, it always helped to talk to Mum and Dad about Rosie and to look at photos of her."
Dan

"What can I do to make the painful feelings go?"

One of the best things you can do when you are grieving is to talk to people, especially family and friends who are close to you.

Being close to the people you love can help, as well as talking about the person you have lost. Don't be afraid to ask for a hug. Some children also like to sleep near to their parents for a while after a death in the family.

Everyone likes
a hug to cheer them up.

It can be very hard to say just how you are feeling. You may find it helps to do a drawing or a painting.

A long walk with your family helps, too, or you may just want to play a computer game and forget about how you feel for a while.

Talk about it

When someone you love dies, you may feel really angry, guilty or frustrated. That's normal, too. Talk to an adult about how you are feeling. If you feel really mad, it can help to:

• Punch a pillow
• Scream really loud
• Tear up old newspapers

"Do you ever feel better after someone dies?"

People do feel better after someone dies, but it takes time. You may never stop missing the person who died. But you will feel better slowly, especially if you share your feelings with others. Some people find their beliefs help them to deal with death.

Let people close to you know how you are feeling.

Just because you stop feeling sad most of the time, it does not mean you've stopped caring about the person who has died.

It's okay to start having fun again, and to make new friends. It can be a good time to take up a new sport or hobby.

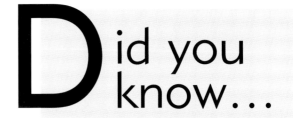

Did you know…

Even when you have come to terms with the death of someone close, special days like birthdays can bring painful feelings back. It can help to remember the good times you had with the person who died.

"What if someone I know is grieving?"

When someone in your family or a friend has lost someone close to them, it can be hard to know what to say to them. You may also be confused because they are behaving very differently. Perhaps a friend at school does not want to join in your games. Or maybe a parent gets angry with you for no reason.

When people are grieving, they may behave differently.

It isn't easy, but don't be sad or angry at them. The person may not be themselves. They may also be feeling lonely.

If you find it hard to say something to them, you can let the person know that you care by helping them in some way.

My Story

"My Mum died last year. I was away from school for a few weeks, and when I went back, I didn't feel like joining in. A couple of days later my friend Josie came up and asked if I was okay.

At first, I just burst into tears. Then I told her all about what had happened. It was really good to have a friend to talk to."

Kathy

"What if I'm upset by something I see on TV?"

If you see something terrible on the television, such as a disaster or an accident which has killed lots of people, you may find that it upsets you.

Even though you don't know anyone who was hurt, it can still make you feel sad or worried. It can make it hard to go to sleep or give you nightmares.

If something on TV upsets you, talk to an adult about your worries.

It helps if you talk to an adult about what you saw and how you feel. Tell them if something is worrying you.

Remember that many things that appear on the news are very unusual and will never happen to you or anyone you know.

Did you know...

If you see something on the news that you don't understand, your Mum or Dad may not know all about it either. You could ask them or your teacher to help you find out more about it.

"Why is death so difficult to talk about?"

Death is such a difficult thing to talk about that grown-ups sometimes use other words to describe it. They may say that the person who died has "gone to sleep". What they are really saying is that the person died peacefully. But no one dies from going to sleep, so don't be afraid to go to sleep yourself.

When we understand what has happened, it is easier to cope with painful feelings.

Adults may say also that someone who has died has gone away for a long time. This can leave some children thinking that the person has run off without them, or that they will return one day.

If you are not sure what has happened, ask an adult you trust, such as your Mum or Dad.

Think about it

We can all cause a death. It can be an accident, such as forgetting to feed a pet, or deliberate, such as stamping on an insect. However it happens, it is important to think and talk about your feelings when this happens, so that you can get to know yourself better and be in control of the choices you make.

What can I do?

• It is normal for people to react in very different ways to the death of someone close to them.

• Crying helps people get in touch with their feelings. If you feel like crying, that's okay.

• If someone you love has died, you will know it can be hard to say what you are feeling.

It might be that you need to hold someone closely.

• However you feel, if you can talk to someone you trust about it, it will probably help.

• If someone you know is grieving, they may behave differently. Try to be patient, and let them know that you care.

Books

If you want to read more on the subject, try:
The Fall of Freddie the Leaf by Leo Buscaglia
(Henry Holt & Co.)
Sad Isn't Bad by Michaelene Mundy
(Abbey Press)
Help Me Say Goodbye by Janis Silverman
(Fairview Press)
What on Earth Do You Do When Someone Dies?
by Trevor Romain & Elizabeth Verdick
(Free Spirit Publishing)

Useful addresses and phone numbers

If you can't talk to someone close to you, then try ringing one of these organisations. They have been set up to help you:

Childline
Tel: 0800 1111
A 24-hour free helpline for children. This number won't show up on a phone bill.

Childhood Bereavement Network
Tel: 0115 911 8070
A national network of support services.

Cruse Bereavement Care
Day By Day Helpline: 0870 167 1677
A national charity offering counselling to bereaved people.

On the Web

These websites are also helpful. You can get in touch with some of them using email:

www.childline.org.uk
www.kidshealth.org
www.rd4u.org.uk
www.winstonswish.org.uk
www.kidshelp.com.au
www.ncb.org.uk
www.dougy.org

Winston's Wish
Tel: 0845 20 30 405
Support, information and guidance for those caring for a bereaved child.

Kids Helpline, Australia
Tel: 1800 55 1800
A 24-hour national helpline offering advice for children.

National Centre for Childhood Grief, Australia
Tel: 1300 654 556
A charitable organisation addressing the needs of bereaved children.

There is a lot of helpful information about grief and loss on the internet.

Index

Photocredits
Abbreviations: l-left, r-right, b-bottom, t-top, c-centre, m-middle
Front cover, 16 — Stockbyte. 1, 28 — Select Pictures. 2, 3tr, 3mr, 6, 10, 11, 14, 19, 22, 24, 26 — Digital Vision. 3br, 7tl, 8, 9, 13tr, 15, 17, 21, 23, 27tr, 30 — Corbis. 4 — Flick Smith. 5, 13bl — Digital Stock. 7br — Corel. 12, 25, 29 — PBD. 18, 20 — Roger Vlitos. 27bl — Brand X Pictures.